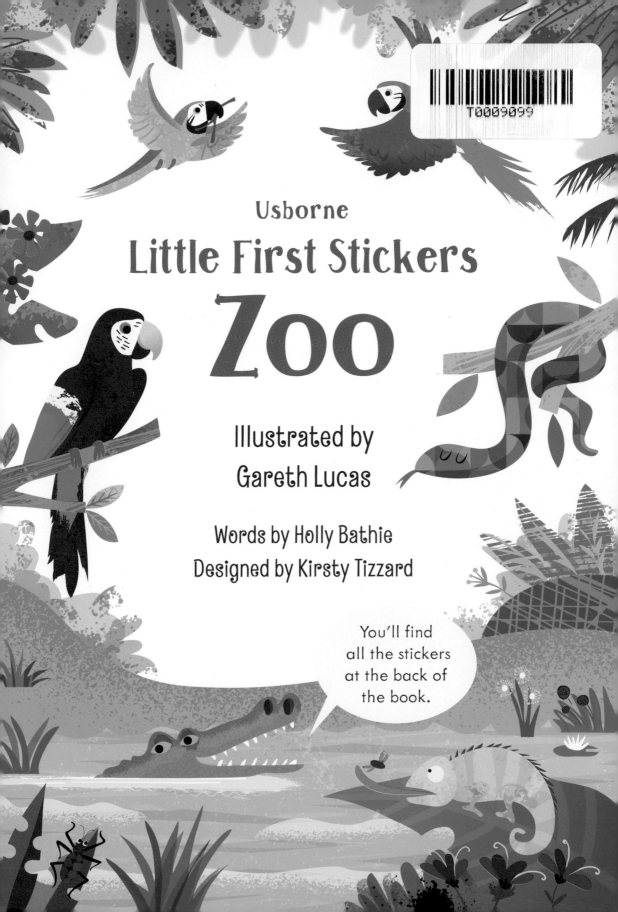

Usborne

Little First Stickers
Zoo

Illustrated by
Gareth Lucas

Words by Holly Bathie
Designed by Kirsty Tizzard

You'll find
all the stickers
at the back of
the book.

Monkeys

These little capuchin monkeys and squirrel monkeys are from South America.

This branch is the perfect spot for a monkey to take a nap.

Stick on some more squirrel monkeys swinging up high.

Add some monkeys eating fruit.

3

Sea lions

Sea lions are clever and can learn tricks.
They are also noisy when they growl
and bark to each other.

Put some sunbathing sea lions on the rocks.

Stick some sea lions on the
platform, eating their fish.

Penguins

You can recognize Humboldt penguins from the pink patches on their faces and feet.

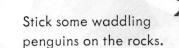

Stick some waddling penguins on the rocks.

Fill the pool with lots of penguins swimming.

Giraffes and zebras

Giraffes and zebras come from Africa. They are herbivores, which means they only eat plants and grass.

Add some more zebras nibbling the grass.

Stick on a family of
giraffes eating the hay.

Find another sleeping zebra
to stick next to this one.

Lions

Lions live in groups, called prides.
They can run fast and roar, but
they also sleep a lot.

Put a roaring lion
on this rock.

Add another playful
lion cub in the grass.

Tigers

These tigers are from Asia. Tigers like to keep cool by the water. In the wild, their stripes make them harder to spot in the long grass.

Stick on a tiger hiding in the bushes.

Add a thirsty tiger drinking from the pool.

Elephants

These are African elephants. Elephants look after each other in family and friendship groups, called herds.

Young elephants like to play in the water.

Add some elephants playing with sticks.

Crocodiles

These are freshwater crocodiles from Australia.
They live in rivers, pools and swamps.

Find two
turtles to stick
on these logs.

Add some more crocodiles hiding in the water.

11

Parrots

Parrots are clever birds, and they squawk loudly. They like to spend time together in groups, called flocks.

Fill the treetops with chattering parrots.

Stick two
sleeping parrots
on this branch.

Aquarium

Lots of different types of fish and other animals
live in tropical waters. Here are just a few.

  Stick some starfish and sea anemones here.

Reptiles and amphibians

Reptiles have dry, scaly skin. Frogs are amphibians; they can live on land or in water.

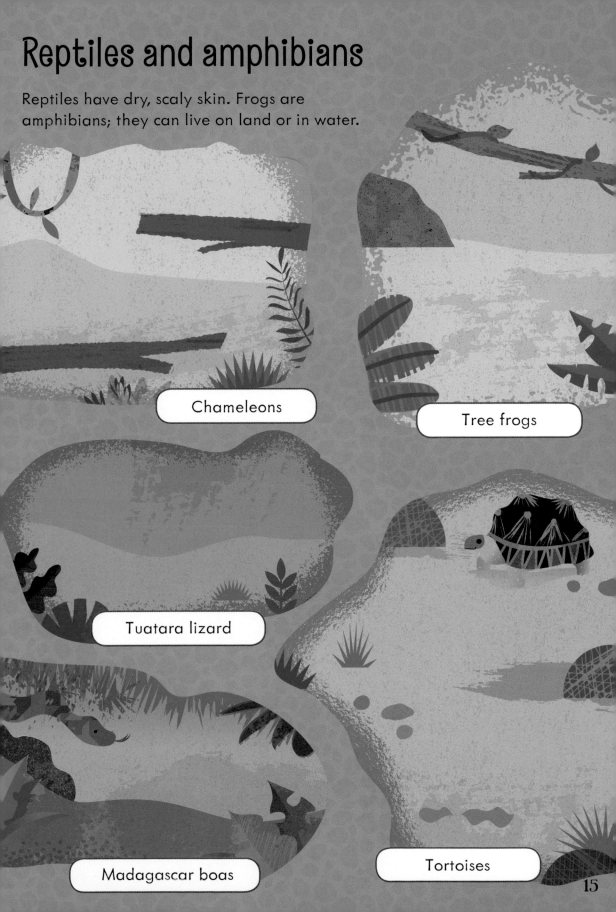

Chameleons

Tree frogs

Tuatara lizard

Madagascar boas

Tortoises

Flamingos

Flamingos are born with dull feathers, which turn pink from the types of shrimps and other food they eat.

How many flamingos are standing on one leg?

Monkeys pages 2–3

Squirrel
monkeys

Capuchin
monkeys

Sea lions page 4

Penguins page 5

Giraffes and zebras

Giraffes

Zebras

Lions page 8

Tigers page 9

Elephants page 10

Crocodiles page 11

Turtles

Parrots pages 12–13

Aquarium page 14

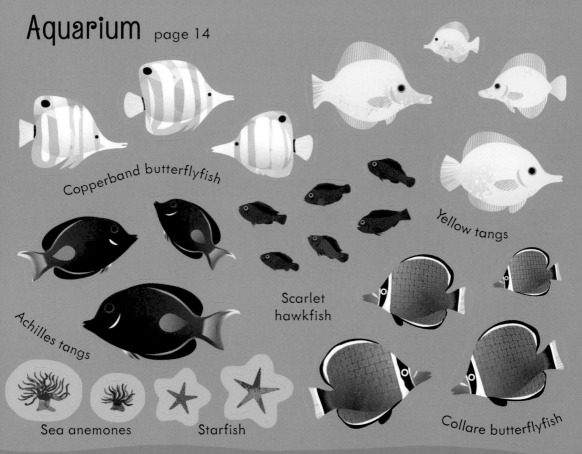

Copperband butterflyfish

Yellow tangs

Achilles tangs

Scarlet hawkfish

Sea anemones

Starfish

Collare butterflyfish

Reptiles and amphibians page 15

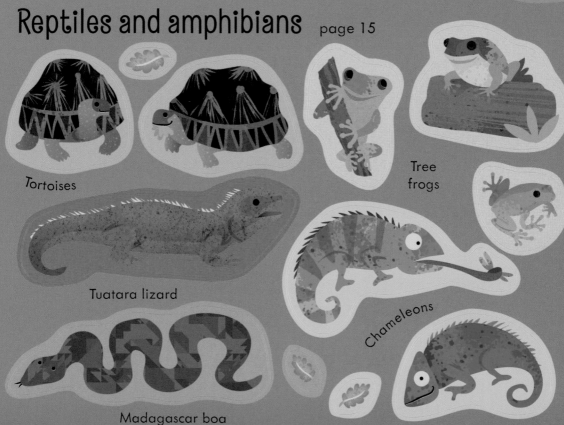

Tortoises

Tree frogs

Tuatara lizard

Chameleons

Madagascar boa

Flamingos page 16

You could put these stickers anywhere in the book.